JOURNEY SONGS

JOURNEY SONGS

KEVIN GIRARD

Library of Congress Control Number:		2023923487
ISBN:	Softcover	979-8-3694-1297-8
	eBook	979-8-3694-1296-1

Print information available on the last page.

Rev. date: 12/08/2023

To order additional copies of this book, contact:
Xlibris
844-714-8691
www.Xlibris.com
Orders@Xlibris.com
857210

CONTENTS

DEDICATION

I dedicate this book to my sister Jacqueline for her untiring support of love and care. She has been there for me time and again. After my parents she has been my best friend. I will always be grateful to her without which this book would not be possible. Thank you, Jacqueline.

ACKNOWLEDGEMENTS

I must acknowledge the kind support of the Iris Court staff. They read these poems and told me what they thought. The book would not have been possible without their technical support and encouragement. In particular to my friend Abdirahman Warsama who made me feel that these poems were good and they had something to say to a wider audience. He inspired me to go on. Thank you Abdi. A friend be.

A PHARISEE

An inside turned out.
Words that do shout.
Beauty of detail, words of fact.
Listen to me, Proud I be.
Humility I did not see.
Images, fantasy; times past.
Impressions thought would last.
Naked of soul. A movement of the whole.
The Will did not sign.
No contract hidden by the mind.
Body did hide the interior inside.
Technology did reach
Deep within, broke my sleep.
Was I alone no more.
Had eyes of hunger
and bedroom size.
Sex did reach but incomplete.
Fantasy of the mind not a body reality.
Viral is the claim, it is in vogue.
I did not say know.
Beats of the heart, trips of the mind
Leave values behind.
Pride be the course
Becomes status lost.
Rejected by the Son.
Blinded by the animal one.
Relate before it's too late.
Fair beings of beauty care.
Dream, fantasize - who would care?

Internal disarray but does not stop the say.
It did not match, flame burned wood;
One's power could not, but what of despair?
Realized loss of one's hair.
Cover no more from the Son.
Bedrooms of fantasy - ceilings of glass
hide not one's heart before.
Before it's too late
change one's state.
Date online, porno - did make horno.
Run by the body of water with no depth
Surface dwellers come together
no celebration - humanity no longer.
Once more dignity lacks true colour.
Humility brings dignity.
Dignity of the mind lost somewhere far far behind.
Clouds move in judgment day.
Choice to make. Can I make the brake?
Pull up my pants give up the naked dance.
Pity me not. But please; put me on the spot.
A culture of pleasure sought.
Death be everyones lot.
Park your car - one day won't start.
Simplicity of a tree - unity of the Three.
Valied threats have customs bought.
Friend of the scribe - what do they describe? Say hi!
Think of the trees – God moved not with
Out of here yesterday become be gone-
leave behind seeds of trees - but are they too old.
Youth sought - pictures of that which is left behind.
Suffering did choose - what was there to lose?
Disunity of body and soul which now define.
No more words - actions to behold.

Safety not did find
capture pulsing's finger touch
I did not see the disruption inside.
Never too late remember Grave Matters.

November 27th 2023

A ROSE IS A ROSE

Watch words that say
"My heart has moved away"
Pretty face to see.
An elegant body
Eyes that glow
All to real nothing show
Hands have not touched.
But the rose has my heart touched.
A flame maybe not
A joy to be given a place
A place to share.
A place but I wont stare
Choices are free.
As of yet she has not rejected me.
Beauty in full bloom
In her heart is there room?

September 24, 2023

ALL TOO CLOSE - A POEM FOR A FRIEND?

Trees of the forest, who can see?
Birds fly between like messages heard and greet.
What to say?
No finger touch
Is coffee too much?
Words written on the page cannot reality is to explain.
Years shared.
Not different but the same.
Like flowers in the field fair faces – wind does blow,
Is this the movement of a heart?
Does the one now look back at the inside,
A reflection of a broken mirror?
Serious to the sound fear not it is not a desire to shame.
Freedom is the call
Choice of the same.
Fear not. Nothing is aflame.
Changes only thee can tell the sharer of Art.
Location is sought tell the art.
Enough of their leaves that fall at ones feet.

September 22nd, 2023

ACT OF SUFFERING

Seek Cardinals.
Birds of freedom.
Strength of heart.
Character do they come to part.
A person does impart.
Virtue to be sought.
Go become the One>
> Another one>
> Be like the Son!
Say fast until it will last.
Bricks they lay foundation is the relay.
Personal within control
This is so for the walk the journ'!
Vow to battle.
Courage is the metal.
Marriage is one battle.
Vowed obedience – freedom of persons found.
Over and over choose the one.
No other one – challenge be.
Hold together is love,
Not pleasure.
Pleasure is the gift of love.
Marriage of love finding pleasure.
Holy is the choice of few.
But beauty is what come up blue.
Clear and eyes of true.

Simplicity is the call.
Stand tall.
Life's foundation is the Art of Suffering.
That's reality – Solidarity.
Choose Life.

November 11, 2023

AWAKENINGS

From sleep did wake.
No longer could wait.
Personal maybe but it was important to quake.
One's life was at stake.
Discussion did tell
Insecurity Fell,
Heard the internal bell.
Passion would rise I did not realize.
Once concern with personal size.
Accepting now
But did it come how?
Short time - needed experience wow.
Learn to release.
Now found peace.
Pluck a flower Love a Sparrow.
Hit by an arrow.
One fell silent not sorrow.
The journey begins - no longer heart hollow.
Self pleasure did one seek.
Deep Did I speak.
Text did pay
All in the name to say.
Many a Nightingale.
Out on the ocean did my ship sail.
No longer impart forgiven thought.
One said never nought.
Until on the spot.
But did not contract sign.
Thrown a life line.

Delete all that was App.
It was draining the sap.
Dreaming of the act.
Saved by the holy.
Words spoken to the lonely.
Once known to the only.
Choices made.
Consequences dismayed.
Possibility laid.
Freedom bought.
Peace of Mind sought.
Sermon on pharisee.
Made me again see.
Hidden by a door
But dreams of a score.
Time now take in hand
Choose the everyday bland.
Get up on your feet and stand.
Dignity now the lay of the land.

November 7, 2023

BLUE SKY

Running under blue sky
You know word of a lie.
What is it you're looking for?
In a boat can you reach shore?
See her before
Touched by a hand
Have you reached dry land?
Understand flowers as they stand
Sparrows do abound.
Stay on solid ground.
Turn, turn, and turn around
Pictures of beauty do see
Can they see inside me?
Are they free?
Birds of the air faces fair
Of course I care.
Some be aware
Profile check
Play chess – check mate.
Simple as it sounds.
Hear the Nightingales song sweet all around.
Here the sick better found
Will they see broken humanity?
Secrets will be hidden unti alll that is left, sterility.
Try as you might - is there a believability?
Among a field of flowers the heart they can devour.
Fear not - be bold it is your hour

Do not let it sour
Compassion is like a tree
Leaves on branches for all to see
Will you friend be?

October 19th, 2023

BRIDGES TO CROSS

Journey begin immitation to Behold.
Stones are problems told.
Dark shadows incomplete
Wholeness, unity, purpose be?
Found, not sure?
Reflect on Scrip'
More than words to see.
Live life as a parable.
Choices to make
Fear not the mistakes.
Many bridges ahead
Lessons from the dead.
The way of love and freedom
Essence is liberty.
One will choose the good.
Cry out from the silence.

October 2nd, 2023

CHOICES FREE

Consequences not.
Put you on the spot.
Do you learn and get taught?
Jump down - leap of faith.
Ground you walk on
Is it sound?
Family part of the game?
Single and no shame.
Celibate be.
Don't live in a tree.
Choice made - you are free.
Can look bodies can see.
Touch not oneself.
Read the books on the shelf.
Only gain spiritual wealth.
Still pass the physical health.
Nourished by the body.
Tradition one has
Life is not put on pause.
Look at the clause.
Vows did make at heaven's gate.
Take a breath but don't wait.
There are those who hate
Act before it's too late.
Love is one's call.
Not a date!
A choice after the fall.
Some a choice from the start the better part.
It was a choice of the heart.

Not to set apart.
The battle has been fought
Victory has been sought.
Alone one not be.
Family is humanity.
Realize this is reality.
Poverty, obedience - chastity
Suffering is the choice
Remember not to lose your voice.
Something to say
Rather than to lay.
Pride is not to be
The choice made through humility.
A choice in time is timeless.
Amount does not have to see.
He does not live in a tree.
Not insanity.
Write on the wings of a dove.
There's not at others in distain.
Only be not the same.
Unique is not the claim.
The persons' call to unity.
Heard in solidarity.
Not an island.
Live with others is where one does stand.
Run the race out of place.
Will not live in other space.
Heaven is the goal.
What is in store?
Nothing more.

November 8th, 2023

COVID

More condition of the mind
There are more than one kind.
Search out self knowledge
Deficiency will be found
immunity will be down.
Interaction must be limited.
Hear voices - or sickness of the mind?
Talking to yourself.
Are you your only friend?
Do you know the shadow of reality?
Does darkness cause shadows to be?
Crushed by thought
Madness sought.
Is it fun to be insane?
Take your meds and don't complain.
Psychiatrist to see
only shadows they see
Talk to me.
Word spoken by the broken.
Wounded humanity.
Fallen pieces where to start
Anguish felt in the heart.
Needing glasses
will they help see the masses?
Dance to the tune
Beat on the drum
Pulsing thoughts come.
Blood rushes to the brain
Thoughts of suicide drain

Will it stop the pain.
Family shame.
Loved one lost
distance does cost.
Embrace the shadow before it's too late.
Like the insane, a mind state.
Does the rhyming make sense?
Build bridges not a fence.
Trust me shadows would take offence.
Turn, turn try to learn
in the mind there is no kind.
Alien but normal.
Journey be - masturbate the mind.
That is a waste of time. Time is the essence
Time demands presence.
A gift of presents
Oneself unwrapped be?
Search out another.
More than a mother
but cannot make connection with other.
So why bother?
Find oneself alone.
Your heart will set the tone - if another found.
Set alarm alone to be
Only then be free.
Is that a possibility?

October 7 2023

DARKNESS RAINS

Water from clouds
Drops in despair
Travel down to the towns
People stand to get wet
Refresh no one because of want.
They hit the ground
Some make sounds when in between.
Not able to forget
Run for cover try forget.
Will clouds relent
hidden is the Son.
What can one expect?
Close me never go, raining down darkness, found run into the past.
Dropped ancient like mistake
into the penalty box.
Only then will clouds go away
In the past stay.
Be a smart fox.
Go to the bank with your deposit.
Vigilant be.
Look skyward and see.
White is snow.
Darkness will rain
Treat with disdain
If not, heart will stain.

Wait, wait for the sky.
With no word lie.
Fragile, soft, depth of soul
Kindness will come with no toll
Fear not One, for they see the Son.

October 12, 2023

DRIFT WOOD

On the ocean see.
Wood drifting to be.
Where it came from.
Somewhere under the sun.
Will it reach shore?
What was in store?
Fallen from a tree.
Cut down by a saw.
Left behind by one so kind.
Be so lucky, picked -up by hand.
Will it reach land?
Was it a race?
Now know one's place.
Water logged.
Heart becomes soft.
To the heights of a loft.
Sink it might.
But no, drift wood floats.
Sparrow left behind.
Ugly wood be.
From a beauty.
Lost at sea?
Home for another bird? Hopefully.
There will be another sparrow.
Shot by an arrow.
Heart sucome.
Nothing more fun.
But reality.
This leaves intact dignity.

Does drift wood have feelings?
A person it not be.
With water dealings?
Carried by wave.
Can another save?
Is there purpose left in me?
Return to one's body.
Dance to the beat.
Listen to the organs.
Whisper sadness in heart.
Quietly, quietly rice paper stand
Running on Ethereal Plains
Nothing more to explain
Treat Meloncholy with distain
Leave one's heart no stain
Eventually come apart.
Doomed from the start
Do what is between
Try not to make a scene.
Be as smart as a dean.
Combination of Co-operation.
Who wood be left?

October 14, 2023
Kevin Girard

FAIR - US - WHEEL

Enter the grounds.
Pay to enter
All kinds of sounds
Many all around
Coming for fun and games
Booths of food, some places beer
Hand in pocket.
Out comes the wallet
Many to share.
Hot dogs, cotton candy, whatever you desire!
Games people play.
Toss a ball, shoot a gun
Chance is slim.
The only certainty is separation from your money.
Now is the time to search for your honey
This is a bee flying from ride to ride
Some look for fun, some scare
hold your breath - need air?
Wait in line
Was it a dare?
Captured by the speed, noise and screams
Experience once or twice
Come back without any advice.
Off you get only to another ride
Chapel on the side.
Here comes the Fair – Us – Wheel.
On you both go - never stop the feeling.
Unity, dignity it's all simplicity
Ride without fear

With the one dear.
Many will leave
Because they don't believe.
They don't believe in the Fair – Us – Wheel.
Around and around
Life will astound
Trinity Bleesed
Out of control
Don't worry It will be best
Together it will last!

October 9th, 2023

GIVING THANKS

Celebration of Kind.
Psychology of wonders.
Stealing nature's thunder?
Important to know –
not just to show.
Celebration why?
Understand the reverly.
Dance no longer, step once more.
Kindly be.
Give the gift of shade of the tree.
Cover the darkness of their reality.
Exclusion of the many.
Television for the few
Doesn't fill the pew.
Smell that which vomit and the stool.
Asking too much of the plenty?
Can they knows?
Bleak is the cover sheet
Covering a song, can you hear the beat?
Once was a Song of the many.
remixed and tranformed into hard knocks.
Anger forgive - poor always with
choose ones not friends of the Son.
Preach beyond the restored.
Open the doors of the grocery store.

Visit the sack and be considerate.
Cloth those with nothing more
Why?
It's on to the Son!

November 28, 2023

GRAVE MATTERS

Coughn' one brings to the fro a life explored
6 feet deep, space it is a relief? Release or no peace?
Above their stand people who look on with grief.
Words spoken from parchment of odes read by a priest
who knew not what was told
he knew not the one now found home in the ground.
Vision of dark that's around not only those who grieve but he the
world did leave.
The question be will he skyward be, released for his sins condemned
to a place in which only darkness and pain reign?
Times untold the words of a shadow who did not know.
What did he not grasp?
Straws, cups, plates did he eat the meal of a good day?
A day coming gone all too short to descend it is all too late.
Midnight begins the rise of shadows face.
One, two, three in the morn' - in the dark one cannot see or feel, all
to unreal.
With dawn - is this a dawn have new grace?
Brought to the new life just beyond nights grasp
Learn from the darkness of the night
The night is darkness-but all too many shadows fall because there is
no light found within
By mid morn', time has been written to that told.
Look not at sorcerer tales of who, hear not a word of no return.
Distance now from darkness that did unfold an ode written in words
of a life's disgrace
Expected more, travel a past all too often nothing able to replace
Learned ignorance once is the plight of those who take flight.

Up, up one goes, does nothingness tell a tale to be told?
In the grave is one's soul, of hold, open to reality of light.
Arming oneself with little toys played in yards known only in disgrace.
Two become one lost interior given to each one, between a world of escape from that
darkness that clouds hide shadows joun'.
The plot not told is not for called grave to fools who dance to the tune of the dissent into the ground.
Hands on the deck-shift sail to parts unknown
Wave after wave grief is the cry
Hope to reach the sky.
Spinning and sewing does your quilt cover the dead?
Untruths often told lifes freedom put on hold.
Jackets that are straight bind a life reaching death's gate
Images of times past more fully in the mind of the one consumed by a race lost in place
Many ways to speak words of nothing but nothingness told to that who stand
At the box descending into sand.
Making castles out of sand the ocean tide rushes into cover ones ground to the others below.
Fingers that no longer bring food sustinence sought to find a broken heart
Down, down does to descend the food taken at the very end.
Does one bite, chew or spew that have ones time?
As evening moves in another darkness engaged to a mind home in the grave.
No children to behold-disintegration untold-parts consumed by bugs of times lived in the darkness
conceived in ones mind.
Distance from that of midnight did start

How far from darkness only to descend into a different darkness close in the ground.
Shadows of relations conceived either grief or fear on their own and face
"When will I begin to cough"?

September 20, 2023

IT DOESN'T MAKE SENSE

But it does make cents.
Images cast on a screne
Anchors on ships that float.
Telling tale of woe.
Analyzing people, places and things.
Covering the world with a blanket of word.
On top to share would only scare.
A cast of support it doesn't report.
Editing what to say, what is to be left behind behold?
Do they have interest who watch?
Laying their bodies have evidence scattered around.
Here there is violence to share
Distance by nature well human tragedy
Does it add up?
Professionals they may be.
Looking straight into the lens that projects into objects of release.
Salary of sum.
Why, changing times all too fast?
Face is gone amateur replace - will they last?
For it is important two things:
One: it doesn't make sense.
Two: turn the switch close!

September 25th, 2023

MELONCHOLY

A poem inspired by John Keats

His was an ode called "Ode on Meloncholy"
Mine is called "To Meloncholy"
To marry a Maid whose name is Meloncholy
Is to see Beauty veiled in the dryness of the mind
Dust does roll off from that Witch sends spells on the wings
Of dust into unhidden eyes.
Each spec of dust is a word of hate
Divorce before it's too late.
Beauty first seen like a drug that from needles change thee
Why did one embrace Meloncholys' beautiful breast?
Was it to inspire, to deep in ones' word spoken by the pen?
Deep reaching to deep trample her under your feet
Walk bold, choose right finding inspiration bright
A relation of the misguided seen not because of the dust
Drops, drops a surgeons reply
Eyes to be cleared of Meloncholys' face
Warnings of a dawn misplaced, light unfound darkness all around.
Does pain inspire a depth of ones' being?
But only will be left with nothing but dust.
Take a broom and sweep the floor following not her steps.
Meloncholy is her name don't transfer identity to a change in her
last name.
Seek beauty of waters that are strong and clear ones' mind is dear
Turn away, send away Meloncholys' so called grace.
Don't be the fool ones' art is at stake

September 13, 2023

KIDNEY STONES

Painful be.
Inside they came from thee.
Slowly they grow
Nothing yet show
Not fatal to one
pass them on.
Sickness inside.
Dance to the beat.
Beauty inside one day meet.
Breathe deeply
Without oxygen sleepy.
Filter the blood,
Infection stop.
Important stay on top.
Unity, dignity, cooperation see
Now you can climb a tree.
Ready to take a view
Make sure to wear shoe.
Out on the branch,
Look for those on the ranch.
Riders, horses can see from the tree.
Down one must come to reality
If one does not all will be sterility.
Compassion sought
expressed in thought.
A friend be
Get off your back the monkey.
Only then free!

October 9th, 2023

LOUISE

To Behold the beauty a tale told.
Received natures touch.
Married young years not gone.
A break took place.
Following ones call you flew as a Nightingale.
Hospitals are where you are found.
A turn came, a turn away from grace
Something happened deep within your soul
Soon to be pleasure sought.
Had learned relationship sound - hallways of patients to heal.
Many a skill.
Given to patients a beauty to behold.
Alas a gift to those who were sick.
Kindness, empathy but always a professional be.
Was there a new call?
Did you see it come or did you just fall?
Now it was a drive like a car in the need of gas.
Driving to bodies in houses in places with hungry faces
Was it enough to fill the whole?
At least 8 inches told.
Shared communication was all too often emptiness of soul.
Did you know the outside of your body?
Did you know that beside your body was a soul?
Dancing reveal more than your face.
Eyes of those who cared little for your heart - it was them who beat
To tunes - a winter's song.
Found there the same.
Love was what the exchange?
Years of the same.

Growing dear a baby did appear - but what happened to the little seed?
Looking again to sing the songs of the Nightingale.
Surprise, you saw a patient with beauty in her eyes.
Relationship found.
Now together in a Nightingale's nest.
Years have passed - do you wonder of what has been lived in place to place?
Has a rock been found - a turn of the heart all the same.
Now in forties to be – look forward change lifes call again.
Will you discover the soul within?
Does that matter - can't be seen in other?
The call to reflect
Fly, fly away in search of grace that is my battle cry!
Be that the One.
Something more to replace then driving of the car.
Don't abandon what nature gave.
Just toil and spin to weave a quilt of thread to save.
Covering not bodies who don't explain.
Can my tale be real - or, is it a mystery of the heart in me?
We've never met but images did see.
Hope one day a poem to read.
A lifeline thrown to those struggling in the sea.
Do you care for words of hope?
Has the emptiness not been relevant?
Do you need words of heart?
Have you found your place?
Living a life all people produce art.
On what canvas did you paint?
Was it a portrait bold?
Or the on coming of old?
Judging not now - has sentence been pronounced?
Words to encourage once again a movement of soul.

September 23rd, 2023

MARY

I sing a song to the perfect beat.
"Mary, oh Mary the one whole and complete"
Without mistake a true original.
Born in the far, not past
The time she's timeless.
Times have changed but not your heart.
More than a friend nothing can make me depart
Mother of God
To some too much to say.
Ephasis 431
Doctrine be
Already known by those who care
Nothing new, always been.
Your part in salvation history.
Never left us, you stay
Visiting us you share
Messages of hope
Not just to pope
But to those who need kind words today.
Heart of love no one can compare
Unique be
Have always been free.
Intercede is the cry of ones
Mary, oh Mary home in the sky.
Not just a shadow but body of the Three
Notes of respect.
Love untold but know my love no boundaries to expect.
Soft words cannot express reality

October 5, 2023

NOTHING SOUNDS

Is there something to hear?
No sound to fear.
Words fire too dear.
Steps taken but let not destroy.
Behave and don't become a toy.
The question be – want to see?
Reality?
Kindness found in a tree pain
Living down they fall.
May your heart stall.
Choice taken to no sound.
Silence of the mind.
Destroys the peace of soul.
The development of problems beyond toll.
Don't be a mole.
Do you hear a call?
Which may you go and stay.
Hope of a brand new day.
Devil one day to pay.
Slowly move around don't delay.
Around, turn - answers to be found.
Can you still nothing sound?

November 7, 2023

PICTURES, PORTRAITS, PAINTINGS, PEOPLE, PLEASE

Pictures: a dawn it does arrive, dew on the grass.
Small beings flying in the air captured
On film of the past.
Images brought together by means of the click
Put in a house found in the hearts and minds
Seeking to dispel the limitations of the human
Of what's found internal.

Portraits: a Canvas empty feeling, the art of the day
what is one to say?
"Sit straight, look forward, put on a serene face"
capture facets that which does express
The sadness of interior things that reach out to this place.
Stroke with a brush hair coloured to be close and fair.
Fade what is sad, capture histories to and fro
Person, place, purpose bringing together those of relation.

Paintings: field, mountains, cityscapes reflect on the way to go.
Through a gate in which one finds how to relate,
To that in what does abound.
Reach into that one sees: trees, rivers and streams
Painted with the hair from the top, try again,
Painted out of the human heart.
Distance because they are real, really, really, real.
Paintings travel far
upon sand, land a variety of choices to release.

People: population rises, people see the openings of realities,
of moving close in a small world of place.
Friends, foes together whatever, there is no other.
Those of four legs search to find
Open fields in which to run and to race.
Crowds push, pull, kick and relate
to nothing more, nothing but disgrace.
What to do now?
Please, people, paintings, portraits, pictures–
represents a reality to the two legged one through an eye.

Please: please be real to that does for those found on a tiny ball,
circling in a "system" of stars that lead,
To everyone found in the forest of Grace.

September 11th, 2023

PORTRAIT OF ART

Portraits are a lost Art.
Consciousness of the mind
Depiction of individuality
Source of liberty and life
Science it be not.
Strokes of the brush
Paint the face of relationship
Connected to the other
Linked by hand in touch.
An affiliation of kind
A life lived like Art.
A craft learned
Start with a desire: Art as love.
Background be one
The One be the focus
Colours not the same
Never explain the poor and the rich
Fame is to be explored
Family, oneself, complexity.
All this reality of truth
Honesty is no small part
Understood as sincerity
Judge ones Art by the depth of
Concepts of thought.
Art in belief
A notion of no repeat

Artificial sound.
Heard by no one
Listened by no one
Perceived by few.

November 11th, 2023

PRUDENCE THE CALL?

"calling on all caution"
round and round words of choice
Actions, preferences end picks.
All describe to find the style
All important to ones' decision
Is there a question here?
A doubt in ones' mind.
Over and over and over the habitual life
A state of being, an existence the question see
Power and passion.
Go to with intensity
Infatuation with women
Nothing here wrong
Whispers in marriage pleasure prolonged.
Choose a face - beauty not only to locate
Discover a world governed not by destiny
Do you live in a tree?
Reality: come down to
Establish a choice: righteousness is in place
Simply said. Sorrow is in your head.

November 12th, 2023

REFLECTION

Should some reflect?
To look in a mirror.
Look in still water
What should expect?
Beauty come back
Or run away old.
Old in heart, maybe not in face.
Reflect another who told
Told that of kindness
Or eyes of anger.
Tell the difference and you score.
Points add up in the game of life.
Skating on ice there: one stays cold?
If you see the stands full begin to wonder.
Overwhelmed.
Reality real,
does the crowd hiss and cry?
Cheer you on but all too non reality.
Look inside if your eyes can see,
Do you see inside a heartbeat, or do you listen to the organs
playing tunes of regret?
Wearing no shoes walk a lot.
Bring your heart.
Get off the ice.
Pass the bench the so-called coach will call:
"back on the ice!"
Locker and undress - is there room?
Outside - is there reality to address?
Letter fly to and fro messages of reflection be.

No crowd sickness
Cured by pill
Pills of redress
Does this stop pain of one?
Find that which found. Realize the sky of open sound.
Choose one to be hold.
Not condemn.
Check with family told
Respond to that found.
Exams of outside to correct
Pass or fail
It is all regret.

September 30th, 2023

REQUIEM FOR THE MASSES

Generation lost,
at a terrible cost.
Disconnected from the past.
Buried Tradition with the dead.
Holy Writings lost from head.
Hierarchy a mountain climbed,
No longer venerated in the mind.
Support one another –
foundation lay in bed.
Anticipate marriage - no dignity of soul to relate.
Spiritual maybe, lost in the sea of lonely.
Is that enough?
Fluff is now the stuff.
Stand in on the play
Words of actors to display.
The audience left because they are deaf.
Nothing more to express.
Ears closed, disrespect.
Community lost in a society with no heart of shared thought.
Communion of the masses insolence taught.
Coming children did stop
Wine reserved for dinner with another time.
Integrity lost. Dignity forgot.
Do questions arrive?
Piety burnt by match.
Married of two.
Homes now described without the Advent
even Yuletide.
Worship by an idol of no tyme; period.

Presence exchange for ones essence by no remembrance.
Hope lost deep. When will be the Fall?!
Technologies spew winter words.
Humanity repressed.
Humility no longer an Art: sought, bought or parking lot.
People run on gas
cars do run from the Son.
Inquiry no longer invest.
Many on the markets the rosary of hand.
Possessions now the definition of the Holy Land.
Death no longer taught,
cut off time; pray not.
Quickly close the door
until relationship with the One restored.

November 18th, 2023

RUNNING ON ETHEREAL PLAINS

What is found? Questions will abound.
Search not one's heart, desception hard to explain
Flowers seen are they visions of beauty?
Springing up thought of marriage to behold.
All to quick to pluck at the petals taken
But leave other with nothing but lost.
Dreams of responding to the one to delicate to believe.
All designed with the hope to find what is inside.
To pull apart from the start
Destruction of the other.
How many petals remain?
Built on ideas of grandure.
There is no support for trees
Only insects on roses tell what seemed too much for the world.
Erect chariots, gather horses of a distant time which is real
They are the only escape
Travelling without horses still, it is the one unreal and all the same.
Accept no gesture of what to gain
An image teaching untruth
Classrooms full of beings to distant to see the world that be.
Planted as a seed can you repeal decisions present?
Grab not the plant, pull out, lose identity.
Words to long did a book read lead to the dead daisy?
Was now the stem to weak to suppoort even the softness of their
beauty?
An image of a woman fair
Damaged by the runner

All others wish for wind and rain
Now to the surface the affect of is ethereal but plain.
Embrace the hand reach out to greet before its to late.
Declare defeat!

September 16, 2023
Kevin Girard

SIMPLY SAID WORDS OF NOTHINGNESS

Beauty found, sing Song of Songs to the one where beauty has fed the
Hearts and minds of beautiful bodies that words of nothingness give
meaning
To the glow.
Love does quake fearing feelings too much, run quickly and embrace
Eyes of stories told of hidden feelings brought to the fore
Engaged joy fears times of rage.
Say now without fear vows of grace.
Discovered that forests tell and speak not of future fall.
Leaves from trees dance as they fall grasp hands but don't leave
The air that is shared gives lifes breath to a world of no despair.
Nothing of shame little feet come out
This the reality of beauty not the beast.
Two beats same brought together by what is same.
Difference does abound only to be discovered lost because their
beauty
Of two who did meet saw difference to seek.
The northern sky led by signs of that will reach back to the places
found in spaces.
To and fro the legend will grow.
Tales of travel steps taken and trails will lead even to the old.
Painted by brush on an empty canves – portraits of beauty to behold.
Daily say prayers to the tunes found in the Song Of Songs relationship
to be
Proud of what was found.
Sleep tight it is now night

September 14, 2023

THE FALLING OF WATER

From how far up, does it start?
It flows down like sad thought
Clear and in some places cold.
Voice of despair, all too often shared.
Does the water speak of where it came from?
Falling onto waters still.
It disturbs the waters below.
A mind left bare. Over waves from mountains home.
Between the waters escape.
Thought that does stream.
How deep into the still waters below.
Does it fall on stones?
Whose problems declare?
Does it hurt to fall on stones?
Back up it cannot go.
Evaporating water, rise to the sky.
Is this lie a release?
Seek not the soothsayer of so called truth.
Pool one's thought swim from side to side.
Water will fall.
Are there waters with whom you care?
Receive the water given.
Hope can be found out of the ocean sound.

September 28th, 2023

THE INDIGENT

Hidden by clouds of no address.
Poor without purpose,
Begging to be heard
Invisible because of no touch.
Obscured by the property mind.
Veiled words of no respect.
Humanity no longer but dignity bought.
Rectitude of the few
The question be: righteousness for the lost?
Cut off as branches from a dead trees.
Burned in the eternal fire - match lit by the few!
Get to the root of instability.
The upper class taught on stupidity.
Markets of the mind; tools of no kind.
Quotes dance of repeated law; impunity sought.
Rights of the one; wholeness the lost.
Viral words have no coherence
Province of edicts
Proclamation of currency
Inclusion lost.
The spread of food lack structure
dispensation deconstruct with intent.
Will government repent?
Carts for the bottles in the bank no deposit.
Indigenous of despair
Unequal by the eyes of disrespect.
Compassion is the call:
forgotten after the Fall.
Begging for an answer

In search of bathrooms: the way of the Cross.
No steps taken to redress the oppressed
Living in glass houses
Fear of the many throwing stones
Sorry not enough
Quickly they grab their stuff.
Banks of food: Workers of the poor
Children rip from feeding breast.
Mother Church speaks for the rest.
On the horizon is the Son
Judge of the disrespect.
Contradiction of a life chosen
With poverty in eye's sight.
Choice of displacement
Found in the basement.
Under frames of oppression
No one ever learned the lesson.
Always be - cry for restored dignity!

November 24th, 2023

THE MICROPHONE

The battle is engaged.
Hurry up on stage.
Perform in the middle of the storm.
Act your own age.
With one's voice enrage.
End of paper spoken word, when?
Sing like a beautiful bird
Choose a Nightingales word.
Bring the people along to the steeple.
It is no trick, don't beat with what is heard.
Question Be - will they have learned?
So pull up your pants be strong.
What to say? All too often one does stay who is
Message of a past relay.
It is now time to start.
Go to the mic ride there on your bike.
Leave behind and depart.
Follow movements of the heart
Can one be? Can one see?
Places to go people to meet on the drum beat.
Nothing is silent when spoken by to those you meet.
Only now say when?
Sit on an egg stand on your leg.
A voice to find.
Be ever so kind.
Travel by wind on the wings of wind.
Look deep think of words to begin.
Listen to the voice heard.
Take your meds and go to bed.

Do not let them disturb.
Anger unheard.
Pick up a stick.
Beat the drum of the Son.
Is the battle won?
Audience with mouths agape - fill the gap.
Be nothing less then wise.
It's not the intent for them to despise.
Parchment do use do not lose.

November 9th, 2023

TO LIVE IN AN AQUARIUM

To live on earth, one is covered by sky.
Cities, Towns, hamlets and cabins are under sky.
Nothing to fear. Air is pumped to those who are dear.
Different be the plants are nothing real.
The fish are real.
All different shapes colours and hungers
But they eat all the same.
People eat differently.
Like there are different shapes colours and hungers,
Like fish if given enough food they would eat until they die.
A weighty matter.
Arthritis in their knees.
Stop the pain please.
To live long medicine is the call.
Weight now – is it to late to repent?
Every while drawn and filled with new.
In houses this is known as spring cleaning
Windows all around.
Look out, one may on glass bump and play.
In aquarium there is no place to go.
All too real – a reality that the fish know?
People are not fish.
Freedom through freedoms choice free.
Breakups many of relationships, unfortunately.
Whether a marriage gone awry or leaving home behind
Unlike fish, we have world of choice.
Start again, build a foundation new
The only question, who's fault?
Can't answer the question?

Then one is a fish trapped within an aquarium.
Bump into the glass, choice is bad.
One is condemned to repeat.
Declare defeat!
The only out of the repeat:
Trust tradition live and told.
Fight for relationship sound,
Find foundation on the ground.
The other choice is damage to the soul.
Any aquarium, the fish have no choice.
Relationship is cold and as water from the tap on the right
Running water is the plight
Tap left.
In the aquariums of the world we look out
do we see ground, people, or trees?
Questions will abound? What have others of free choice found?
Start at the beginning, every once in a while, look back.
What was the choice made?
If it is jobs that are, if necessary, run a way.
It is freedom, to give choice to last
The last choice is to give up choice
To make no choice is a choice
Only the strong can give away choice.

September 28th 2023

TO UNEARTH TIMELESSNESS.

Appreciated by generations.
Visions of a land Long ago solicited.
They View with a desire to Perceive.
Antiquity.!
Is there something? To learn from the past.?
Like wind that blows
Thoughts of the old.
Stand tall, be a Roman.
Is that the call?
A poem to reveal all that is immaterial.
Are words Inconsequential?
Strength of one's kind.
A people to repress? A state of being.
Less to learn. - A shame.
The art. To realization.
Forfeit your right.
What is left?
Shovel in hand.
Earth to move soil to be Assessed.
Failure to prompt a renewal.
Strength of plot.
Hard to find.
Only missed if you try.
An adventure to be true.
A portrait of lost Art.
Character to behold.
Quality that will last.
Look deep inside.
See More Than the Organized?

Thunder down – download but miss, and suffer a toll.
It would be a duty,
Responsibility is one's own.
Unlike Grace It can be fought for.
Tools in hand.
Vibrate not.
Virtue to Be pursued and conquered.
Take seriously.
Solemnly swear.
Do you claim no shame.
Problem is – being?
A People left to exam – did they fail?
A mass of activity. A waste of time?
Strong enough to go to Mass?
Stain of soul and regret.
A reality of disGrace.
It is formidable.
Choose to stand show some countenance.
Join with the vulnerable.
Suffer. Do you know what?
Ignominyness.
Look hard, You ought.
Look in a book.
Sweep off the dust.
Work one must.
An attitude.
Your not in a plane too high.
Be cautious,
But wait. The battle must be won.

November 14th. 2023.

TWO

Separation Be not of the heart.
Struck by love from the start.

Humility is to be the state of how to relate.

Moral yes - but is it truth?
Engage the youth.

A beacon under a tree.

Message of relief.
Embrace the belief.

It can be done all because of the Son.

Touch oneself; images of regret.
The soul is left upset.

Unto the desert the message.

Unto - death embrace.
Leave the trappings of the race.

Reality, not Art plays a part.

Cover ones head.
Make sure not dead.

Live life without strife?

Mind - a life sought.
What should be fought?

Change one or two, that you know.

Virtue or vice.
My life's food, spice.

Love her in bed Choose not dead.

Mind, will, and conscience – a Trinity.
It is all about liberty.

Seek not pleasure that displeasure.

It is to climb a mountain fast.
Is the only thing that will last.

November 11th, 2023

WORDS AS SWORD

To explain, to describe with writings of scribe.
Modesty to be found?
Humility must be sound.
Speak of the journey from pen to page:
images appear, metaphor declare
The word sword scare.
History, philosophy, theology are your friends.
Friends demand honesty
Pass the letter live life be.
Not a science but art
Because it must come from the heart.
To be profound is to be silent.
Nothing more to say.

October 2nd, 2023

WORDS TO ATTEND

Released from the heart, distance fair greeted by ears to attend.
Nature explored, a forest to encounter, do you believe in the reality
of trees?
Leaves fall to the ground like words the other has not found.
A desire to share.
Are the Spirits the source and sway of tainted thought?
Or do the muses of impression move one to explain a world outdoor?
Exchange a word delicate to the flame
Eyes closed, winter of tales led one to woe.
Trees of reality, a forest can see,
do the leaves shade those with heart?
Is the mind one's only source.
Crippled hands cannot softly touch.
Touch: Odes, Sonnets, Ballads and simple poems designed to be
beauty
Be fearless in objectivity
Plan, but less is more.
Be and search spontaneity.
Schools of thought cannot get that which is to be sought?
Unity, depth of being whole.
Can one interpret the words of Grace?
Eternity is the goal.
Bound by words spoken in air
Build a nest in which to find rest.
Once fly from tree to tree, now home is reality.

November 19, 2023

A WORLD BEHIND THE DOOR

Moderation is the call.
Equilibrium Is to be sought.
What is your world behind the door?
Realm of the Insane.
Simple words do explain.
Animal instincts to claim?
Furniture in the room.
Swept and clean.
What does that mean?
Books, chairs, shelf to share.
A bed to share.
Above instincts declare?
More than abstinence.
Abnegation of the instincts.
At the level of the willing to be one of gratification?
Humanity, dignity the cost.
Reality of the body lost.
Realm of the animal – do you no restrain?
In a room a bed lay.
Nothing more to declare.
Central to self-control? The bed of disdain.
Which is the door to be explored.
Room has a world to one.
Mistaken belief - this the freedom of choice?
Harsh words all the same.
All seems simple in the universe of the insane.
Is this a new doctrine of demand?

Claim once more the body of the beautiful.
Sum - more than breasts, Lips and vagina be.
Is that all he sees?
In a room behind the door - A soul.
But one can destroy the heart.
Introspection of the One?
Open the door.
A real world to explore.
Do you care for the poor?
In your world there is toilet.
The equality of all.
Is it all a waste?
Salvation from the bed.
Only if one uses their head.
Need principles that are found in Logic?
Philosophy of the bed.
Ethics is not a huien cry.
Is your body shaped like a bed?
Dare to ask a question.
Covers: hide the sleep denied
Is this the platform for the bed?
Construct a vision of love.
No more than sex.
How to define relationship?
Sign a contract - Find on the street: intercourse.
Know that you are more than a horse.
All will claim- Freedom of choice?
Driven like a car on gas
Release pollution to the outside.

Temperance simply said.
Scared of the Prudent call.
Lose is the control found in the body's" head".
Did I forget to mention the length of the" head"?

One dare ask a question:
Reality?
Scared of the dead?
Claim this is a phobia.
Sea of the irrational.
Do you think no one knows what goes on behind the door?
We all live under an open sky.
Don't be blind. Don't be mute.
Clean once more? The humanity of the body.!?
Self pleasure of the hand.
Not real - Not of the plan.
No relationship between other ones?
The choice is clear.
Heaven the choice. Or do you choose the Underworld?!

November 20th, 2023.

A REASON TO STAY

Poems one does find
stimulate the mind.
Asking what relationship be?
Can you see the reality?
Birds of the air
Cardinals have no despair.
It's within your grasp
questions that will last.
Read over - find mistake within.
Totality not the claim.
Humility - the flight of no shame.
Given a second chance.
Changing meds freed consciousness.
Gift to the poor in heart
explains where it did start.
The Universal Cathedral writes ancient rhymes.
Monks of transmission is their mission.
Silence of the blank page
scream for letters to proclaim.
Incarnate the One.

November 28, 2023

Printed in the United States
by Baker & Taylor Publisher Services